Natural ⚡ Disasters

Flood!

For my grandchildren—M. D. B.

To Alex—J. G. W.

ALADDIN PAPERBACKS
An imprint of Simon & Schuster Children's Publishing Division
1230 Avenue of the Americas, New York, NY 10020
Designed by Christopher Grassi
The text of this book was set in Century Oldstyle BT.
Manufactured in the United States of America
First Aladdin Paperbacks edition September 2008
4 6 8 10 9 7 5 3
Library of Congress Cataloging-in-Publication Data
Bauer, Marion Dane.
Flood! / by Marion Dane Bauer ; illustrated by John Wallace.
p. cm. — (Natural disasters)
1. Floods—Juvenile literature. I. Title.
GB1399.B39 2008
551.48'9—dc22
2007046409
ISBN-13: 978-1-4169-2553-8
ISBN-10: 1-4169-2553-8
1212 LAK

Natural ⚡ Disasters

Flood!

By **Marion Dane Bauer**

Illustrated by **John Wallace**

Ready-to-Read
ALADDIN
New York London Toronto Sydney

Rain falls.

Snow melts.

Water forms tiny streams.

Tiny streams
join larger streams.

Larger streams
run into a river.

The river gathers
more and more water.

Water spills
over the riverbanks.

Flood!

Sometimes the flood is slow.
Water inches up and up.

It spreads and spreads.
People have time
to get out of the way.

Flood Danger
Prepare to
EVACUATE!

Sometimes the flood
comes very fast.

If heavy rain falls
over a wide area,
a wall of water can come
in a flash.

Rivers give us fresh water.

They help us travel.

Even floods help us.

Floods bring rich soil

to grow crops.

But floods can wash away
farms and homes
and whole towns.

We build dams and levees
to control floods.

Dams also help
keep rivers open for travel.

They give us clean power.

Dams create reservoirs
(**rez**-er-vwars).
Reservoirs give us water
to use and to play in.

Dams hold water

for irrigation (ir-i-**ga**-shun)

to grow crops on dry land.

But dams also bring more people to live near rivers.

When a dam or levee breaks,
water covers the land.

When the flood is over,
people come back to the river.

Some are learning to
rebuild on higher ground.

Interesting Facts about Floods

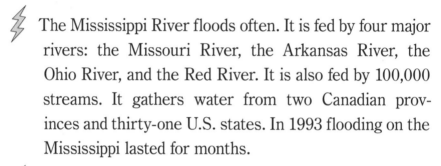

Of the two billion acres of land in the United States, 140 million acres are flooded from time to time.

The Mississippi River floods often. It is fed by four major rivers: the Missouri River, the Arkansas River, the Ohio River, and the Red River. It is also fed by 100,000 streams. It gathers water from two Canadian provinces and thirty-one U.S. states. In 1993 flooding on the Mississippi lasted for months.

The other area of the United States most often flooded is the Central Valley of California.

Water is very heavy. A large bathtub of water weighs three-quarters of a ton. It is the water's weight in a flood that does so much damage.

Dam breaks are one of the most common causes of serious floods.

The National Oceanic and Atmospheric Administration has a National Weather Service that issues advisories. They work to warn people of floods coming. The United States is the only country in the world that has such a service.